KU-350-626

Published in the UK in 1994 by
Schofield & Sims Limited, Huddersfield, England.

All rights reserved.
No part of this publication may be reproduced,
stored in a retrieval system, or transmitted in any form,
or by any means, electronic, mechanical, photocopying,
recording or otherwise, without the prior permission
of the copyright holders.

0 7217 5009 5

©1993 éditions MANGO

Houses

Schofield & Sims Limited Huddersfield.

Dwellings Around the World

1 • A Scandinavian house   2 • A Caribbean plantation residence   3 • A palace in Venice
4 • New York skyscrapers   5 • An English thatched cottage

6 • A timbered house in Alsace   7 • Dutch street houses in Amsterdam   8 • A sampan in Hong Kong   9 • A South American hacienda

3

The Igloo

In the Arctic regions, the Inuit, or Eskimos, set out in winter to hunt seals on the ice-floe. At each place where they stop, they build igloos in which to shelter.

An igloo is built from large blocks of ice which are sawn out of the frozen snow. These blocks are placed one on top of the other, curving inwards to make a domed roof.

The igloo is entered through a passage which is hollowed out under the snow. This tunnel warms up the cold outside air before it reaches the inside of the igloo.

Inside the igloo, oil made from seal fat is used to provide heat and light.

When they are not hunting, the Inuit live in painted wooden houses in small villages.

A Dogon House

The entrance is the husband's room, which has a raised bed of earth where the children sleep at night.

Millet is dried in granaries built of earth. The top of each granary is covered by a 'hat' made of *thatch*.

In Africa, the Dogon people of Mali grow rice and *millet* and raise cattle. Their houses are built in terraced rows. They have flat roofs and are constructed of brick.

The bricks are made from straw mixed with mud. They are then spread on the ground to dry in moulds.

The dead are buried in buildings which overlook the village. The house of the village chief is set apart from the other houses.

The Cave

Prehistoric people lived in caves in order to hide from wild animals and shelter from bad weather. They used twigs and branches to cover the cave entrance.

To protect themselves from the cold, prehistoric cave-dwellers placed flat stones on the ground and covered them with animal skins or leaves. They decorated the walls of their caves with paintings of animals.

Today, some people still live in dwellings that are hollowed out of earth or rock. These houses are reached by steps cut out of the rock-face. Some of the dwellings are several *storeys* high.

9

The Tepee

The tepee was carried on a kind of trailer of poles, called a travois, pulled by a horse.

To erect the tepee, wooden stakes were driven into the ground in a circle, and then fastened together at the top with leather straps.

10

In the past, the Indians who lived on the plains of North America travelled around constantly after the great herds of *bison*. They lived in tents called tepees, which could quickly be put up and taken down.

The stakes were then covered with *bison* skins which had been sewn together. The smoke from the fire escaped through a hole at the top of the tepee.

The inside walls of the tepee were hung with decorated animal skins. The door of the tepee faced the rising sun.

A Pacific Island House

To construct the house, stakes which will support the walls and roof are hammered into the ground. The *framework* of the house is then assembled.

The roof is made from leaves softened in sea water and the walls are made of bamboo.

On the islands in the Pacific Ocean, people live mostly in houses made of bamboo. These houses can accommodate a large number of people.

The house consists of just one large room where all the furniture, the *matting* for sleeping, and the baskets and equipment used for fishing are kept.

Food is not prepared inside the house, but in a special small building nearby.

13

The Tuareg Tent

The furniture of the Tuaregs is very light and consists mainly of decorated or embroidered cushions and pillows, which can be easily transported by camel.

To protect themselves from the wind and sand, Tuareg men wear a veil. They wear this inside the tent as well as outside.

The Tuaregs are *nomads* who live in the Sahara Desert in Africa. They travel about constantly with their camels, goats and sheep. They live in tents made from animal skins.

Near the tent a kind of fireplace is built, usually between three stones. The camels' saddles and the bowls used when milking the animals are hung on the branches of nearby trees.

Tuaregs pitch their tents near to an oasis or a well.

The Yurt

A yurt is made from a *framework* of sticks which are then covered with felt, a thick material made from the hair of sheep or camels. It takes only two hours to build a yurt.

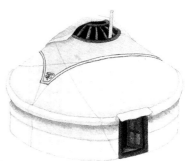

In the centre of the yurt is the fire. Smoke from the fire escapes through a round hole in the top of the yurt.

The Mongols live on the *steppes* of Asia.
They raise camels, horses, cattle and sheep.
They move around with their herds and live
in tents called yurts.

The floor of the yurt is covered with wood, and carpets are laid on top of this. In winter, many thick layers of felt are added to the carpets.

A Japanese House

Traditional Japanese houses have only one *storey*. They are very light and are built out of wood and paper. The roof can be covered with *thatch* or tiles.

The outside walls slide open and the dividing walls inside the house can be removed to form one enormous room. The floor is covered with straw mats called tatamis. You must remove your shoes before walking on the mats. At night, mattresses are spread on the floor for sleeping.

Wooden sandals are worn in the kitchen and the bathroom. The bath is a wooden tub which is filled with very hot water. Before getting in the bath, the Japanese wash themselves.

A Japanese house always has a garden decorated with shrubs, lanterns, stones and sand.

Building a House

An architect draws the plans for a house and supervises its construction.

Some houses are built of brick. The bricks are made from clay which is baked in moulds.

Throughout the world, houses are very different. They can be large or small, built of earth, wood, brick or stone, with or without electricity, gas or running water. But all houses protect us from the weather, and are places where we can relax, sleep, eat and wash.

Nature provides us with stone which can be used to make walls for houses.

To join the bricks and stones together, the builder uses a paste which hardens when it dries. This is called cement.

Houses in Sunny Lands

In sunny countries, houses are often painted white. They are built close together along narrow streets and alleyways to stop the walls from getting too hot in the sun.

The houses in southern Spain are sometimes built around a courtyard, where a fountain and plants provide coolness.

In Arab countries, the windows are protected by carved wooden shutters which prevent the sun from entering.

In desert regions, the houses have few windows so that the interior remains cool. The windows are usually small and narrow.

Inside such houses, the walls are painted white to make it lighter.

Houses Made of Wood

In North America long ago, people were mostly fur trappers and lumberjacks. They lived in cabins made from huge wooden logs. Today, there are still many beautiful wooden houses in America.

The Russian dacha is made entirely out of wood. It is usually decorated with paintings, particularly of flowers.

In the mountains, chalets are made of wood because wood can support heavy loads of snow or ice.

In warm countries, wooden houses are constructed so that rooms are well ventilated.

In marshy regions, houses are built on wooden stilts to avoid *flooding*.

Glossary

Bison
A kind of wild bull with a head covered in curly hair.

Flooding
When it rains heavily, streams and rivers can overflow into the surrounding land. This is flooding.

Framework
The wooden or iron supports around which a house is built.

Matting
Straw carpets which cover the floor of certain houses and on which people sit or sleep.

Millet
A cereal grown mainly in Africa. It is used to make gruel (a kind of thin soup) and flat cakes.

Nomads
People who move from place to place during the different seasons. They do not have a permanent home.

Steppes
Huge grassy plains without trees and with little vegetation.

Storeys
The parts into which a building is divided horizontally.

Thatch
A roof-covering of straw, palm leaves, reeds or similar materials.